Late Elementary Piano Solo

# The Little Drummer Boy

Robert D. Vandall

# The Little Drummer Boy

to lay be - fore the King, pa - rum pum pum pum, rum pum pum pum,
mf
f

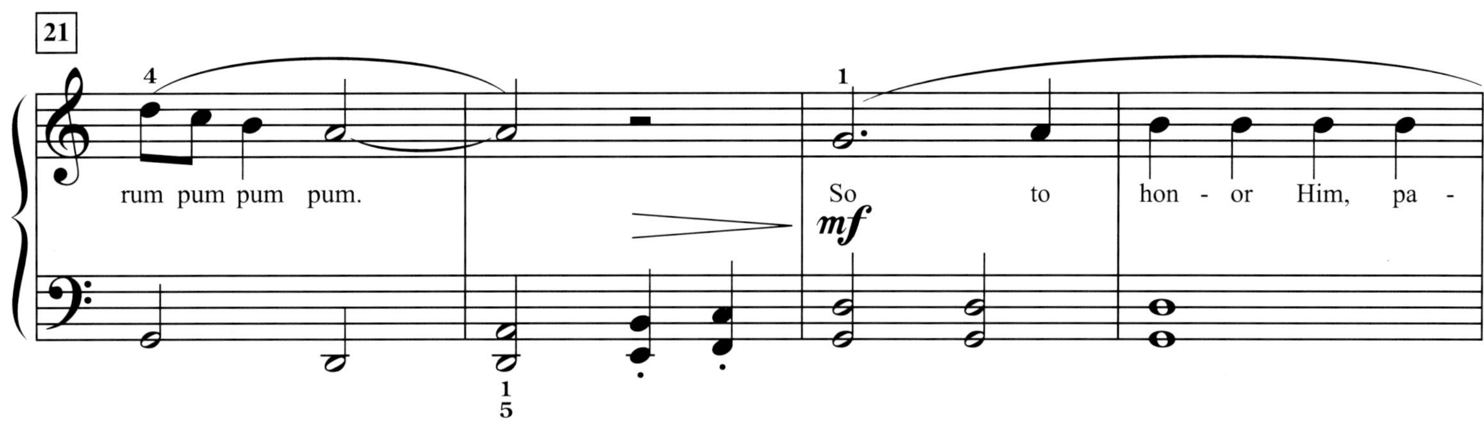
rum pum pum pum. So to hon - or Him, pa -
mf

rum pum pum pum, when we come.
mp

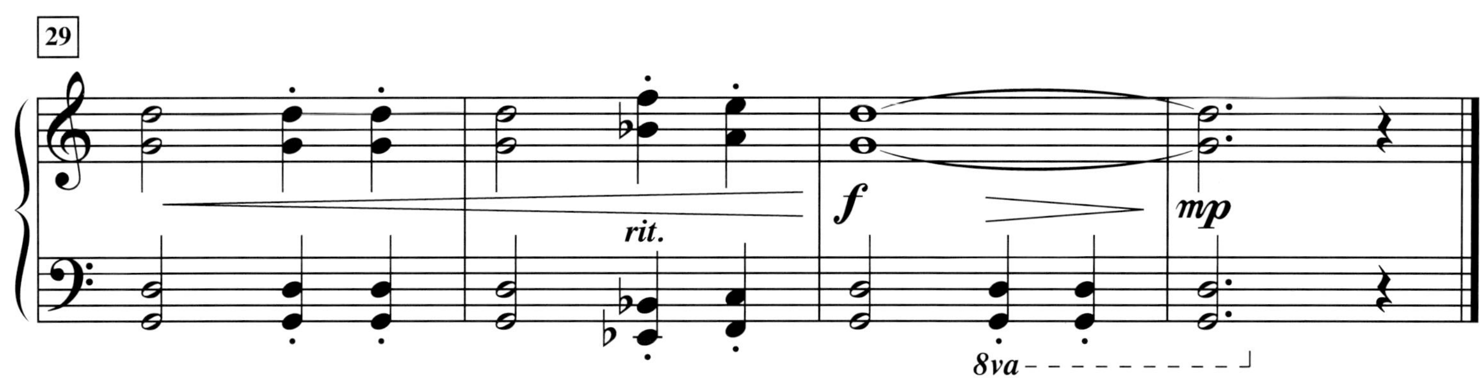
rit.
f
mp
8va - - - - - - - - -

# Alfred's Premier Piano Course

Dennis Alexander • Gayle Kowalchyk • E. L. Lancaster • Victoria McArthur • Martha Mier

**Lesson Book**

| | |
|---|---|
| Book 1A | 22356 |
| Book 1A & CD | 20652 |
| Book 1B | 22358 |
| Book 1B & CD | 22352 |
| Book 2A | 23264 |
| Book 2A & CD | 22173 |
| Book 2B | 25721 |
| Book 2B & CD | 25719 |
| Book 3 | 27779 |
| Book 3 & CD | 30222 |
| Book 4 | 29036 |
| Book 4 & CD | 30202 |
| Book 5 | 30897 |
| Book 5 & CD | 32022 |
| Book 6 | 33919 |
| Book 6 & CD | 34643 |

**Theory Book**

| | |
|---|---|
| Book 1A | 22354 |
| Book 1B | 22174 |
| Book 2A | 22371 |
| Book 2B | 25725 |
| Book 3 | 28040 |
| Book 4 | 30011 |
| Book 5 | 32649 |
| Book 6 | 34668 |

**Performance Book**

| | |
|---|---|
| Book 1A & CD | 21232 |
| Book 1B & CD | 22172 |
| Book 2A & CD | 22368 |
| Book 2B & CD | 25722 |
| Book 3 & CD | 28000 |
| Book 4 & CD | 30010 |
| Book 5 & CD | 32646 |
| Book 6 & CD | 34669 |

**Pop and Movie Hits**

| | |
|---|---|
| Book 1A | 34015 |
| Book 1B | 34016 |
| Book 2A | 34415 |
| Book 2B | 34416 |
| Book 3 | 36431 |
| Book 4 | 36432 |
| Book 5 | 37615 |
| Book 6 | 37616 |

**Technique Book**

| | |
|---|---|
| Book 1A | 27627 |
| Book 1B | 27628 |
| Book 2A | 32077 |
| Book 2B | 32177 |
| Book 3 | 34105 |

**Christmas Book**

| | |
|---|---|
| Book 1A | 30878 |
| Book 1B | 30879 |
| Book 2A | 30895 |
| Book 2B | 30896 |
| Book 3 | 32817 |
| Book 4 | 32818 |
| Book 5 | 36743 |
| Book 6 | 36744 |

**Assignment Book**

| | |
|---|---|
| Levels 1A–6 | 28358 |

**At-Home Book**

| | |
|---|---|
| Book 1A | 22180 |
| Book 1B | 22364 |
| Book 2A | 22365 |
| Book 2B | 25726 |

**Flash Cards**

| | |
|---|---|
| Level 1A | 22355 |
| Level 1B | 22366 |
| Level 2A | 22367 |
| Level 2B | 25727 |

**GM Disk for Lesson and Performance**

*Orchestrations by Brent Mills and Jason Nyberg*

| | |
|---|---|
| Level 1A | 23258 |
| Level 1B | 23259 |
| Level 2A | 23260 |
| Level 2B | 23263 |
| Level 3 | 30426 |
| Level 4 | 30204 |

*General MIDI accompaniments can be downloaded at alfred.com/downloads*

**Success Kit**

Includes Lesson Book & CD, Performance Book & CD, Theory Book, At-Home Book, and Flash Cards in a Zipper Organizer.

| | |
|---|---|
| Level 1A | 23215 |
| Level 1B | 24592 |

**Organizer with Zipper**

| | |
|---|---|
| Clear binder w/pockets | 103595 |

## Universal Edition

The Universal Edition is designed for all English-speaking countries outside of the United States, including Canada, the U. K. and Australia.

**Universal Edition Lesson Book**

| | |
|---|---|
| Book 1A & CD | 23860 |
| Book 1B & CD | 23863 |

**Universal Edition Theory Book**

| | |
|---|---|
| Book 1A | 23869 |
| Book 1B | 23870 |

**Universal Edition Success Kit**

| | |
|---|---|
| Level 1A | 24437 |

39471    $3.99 in USA

ISBN 0-7390-9153-0

ISBN-10: 0-7390-9153-0
ISBN-13: 978-0-7390-9153-1